MANAGING ADHD AS A WOMAN:
Strategies To Coping With ADHD As A Woman

Fiona Robinson

All rights reserved. No part of this publication may be reproduced, distributed, or transmitted in any form or by any means, including photocopying, recording, or other electronic or mechanical methods, without the prior written permission of the publisher, except in the case of brief quotations embodied in critical reviews and certain other noncommercial uses permitted by copyright law.

Copyright © Fiona Robinson, 2022.

Table Of Contents

Chapter 1

Understanding ADHD

The illness known as attention deficit hyperactivity disorder (ADHD) has an impact on how people behave. People with ADHD may appear restless, struggle to focus, and act impulsively. The signs of ADHD are typically identified at a young age and may worsen as a child's environment changes, such as when they start school. The majority of cases are identified in children between the ages of 3 and 7, while this can occasionally happen later in childhood.

Sometimes people with ADHD are diagnosed as adults because they were not diagnosed as children. Although many adults who were diagnosed with ADHD when they were young continue to have issues, the symptoms of the disorder typically become better as people mature. Anxiety and sleep disturbances are two additional issues that people with ADHD may experience. Adults with ADHD may experience issues with:

- Time management, organization, and compliance with instructions.

- Concentrating on and finishing tasks.

- Overcoming irritability or impatience, impulsivity, and risk-taking.

Adults may also experience difficulties relating to others or interacting with others.

ADHD is a widespread disorder that makes it difficult to concentrate, remain still, and deliberate before acting. Some people with ADHD struggle mostly with focus. (ADD is another name for this.) Additionally, ADHD can affect other abilities, such as emotional management.

Differences in the brain are the root cause of the widespread disorder known as ADHD. Focus is a challenge for those with ADHD. But other people are likewise impulsive and hyperactive. This is especially true for children and teenagers. It's unclear just how many Americans are diagnosed with ADHD. However, estimates range from 5 to 11 percent.

Executive function is a set of critical skills that people with ADHD struggle with. And it poses problems in a variety of spheres of life, including employment, school, and daily living. For instance, people with ADHD frequently experience difficulties with organization, following instructions, and mood management. One of the numerous misconceptions regarding ADHD is that it is caused by a lack of motivation or willpower, simply laziness. In actuality, people with ADHD frequently use all of their effort to focus and control their impulses.

For a very long time, it was believed that boys in particular are diagnosed with ADHD. However, evidence indicates that adults also battle with ADHD and that girls and women experience it just as frequently as boys and men.

When people get older, ADHD doesn't magically disappear. Typically, impulsivity and hyperactivity disappears by the time a child reaches puberty, if not a little longer. But focus issues persist. Some individuals don't receive an ADHD diagnosis until after high school or as adults. Regardless of when someone receives a diagnosis of ADHD, some therapies can help manage symptoms. Additionally, some resources help facilitate tasks at work and in school.

There is one perplexing ADHD symptom. People who struggle with concentration most of the time can frequently "hyperfocus" on things they find highly interesting. For instance, a child might concentrate for hours on a craft activity but lose attention five minutes into a homework assignment or an adult could lose track of time because they are obsessively concentrating on a TV show or video game.

ADHD symptoms can appear at any age. Children as young as in preschool can display indications. However, many don't exhibit symptoms until much later, as their workload increases. Some individuals don't recognize they have ADHD until they are in college or the workforce.

The Potential Causes Of ADHD

In recent years, a lot of study has pointed to potential causes of ADHD. According to research on brain imaging, people with and without ADHD exhibit both differences and similarities. Brain growth is fairly comparable. However, in those with ADHD, the regions involved in executive function take longer to mature. Children with ADHD may act up to three years younger than other children their age because of this.

Additionally, research reveals certain variations in how the brain works.

Chapter 2

The Effects Of ADHD On Women

According to studies, women with ADHD frequently have extremely low self-esteem compared to adult men with ADHD, they also appear to be in higher emotional and psychological suffering.

Some women can conceal their symptoms, depending on the degree of their illness to avoid embarrassment and rejection. Others who have ADHD could feel as though their lives are in complete disarray. Since women are often in charge of caring for the home and children, this may have an impact on the entire family according to data.

As a woman, Ineffective coping mechanisms might negatively impact your daily life and amplify your difficulties. For instance, you could find it challenging to manage the obligations of your job, prepare regular meals for your family, or keep up with other housework. Having a constant sense of attempting to catch up might cause chronic stress and tiredness.

If any of these symptoms ring a bell, seek the advice of a medical professional or a therapist, finding assistance should be simpler now.

Currently Doctors are advancing their knowledge of ADHD as a type of neurodiversity. ADHD sufferers are resilient despite the drawbacks. Employers, universities, and other organizations looking to recruit unconventional thinkers are becoming more aware of and enamored with ADHD traits like creativity, empathy, risk-taking, the capacity to think quickly in a crisis, the capacity to work under pressure, and the ability to deeply explore areas of interest.

Thinking of your brain like a fast-driving car might not be the key to overcoming ADHD as a woman. Instead, it's a strong machine that can quickly adapt and learn.

If you are over 50 and were not diagnosed when you were a child or a young adult, identifying ADHD may be challenging due to other health conditions like stress, anxiety, hormonal changes, and even prescription side effects.

The problem of not knowing you have ADHD when you do has a big impact. If ADHD had been identified and treated earlier, it could have been possible to prevent poor emotional health.

Attention deficit hyperactivity disorder (ADHD), which encompasses a complicated grouping of symptoms that affect women and men differently, is estimated to affect 8 million adults (more males than females).

Treatment for women and girls is a specialty of Kathleen Nadeau, Ph.D director of Chesapeake Psychological Services of Maryland in Silver Spring. When women visit Nadeau, she claims that the most frequent phrase they use to describe their symptoms is "overwhelm," which eludes all known treatments and lasts for months or years.

Three forms of ADHD are listed in the most recent diagnostic manuals as; inattentive, hyperactive/impulsive, or a third combination category. ADHD is not a single disorder. The three forms of ADHD are classified using the following diagnostic standards:

Consistent forgetfulness, a lack of focus, an inability to finish activities (ranging from finishing an email to emptying the dishwasher), and an aptitude for being distracted are all characteristics of the inattentive type. Inattentive type ADHD is more frequently diagnosed in adults and females than in males.

Symptoms of the hyperactive/impulsive type can include being extremely chatty, being described as someone who is always on the move or enjoys being constantly busy, as well as frequently feeling restless and fidgety. Boys are more likely to have a H/I type diagnosis.

The traits and behaviors of the combined type, which can range from mild to severe and must become apparent over months or years, might include both inattentive and hyperactive/impulsive traits and behaviors. Most often, inattentive ADHD affects women. Clinicians search for symptoms that are both extremely disruptive at work or home and that continue for extended periods. So, for instance, a ADHD female will forget...but not recognize this as a pattern that is as disruptive as it is avoidable. The average person under stress might forget where they put their car keys or an Internet password.

The experience of ADHD in females differs from that of males due to hormonal systems, which also makes diagnosis more difficult. During critical periods like adolescence, early adulthood, delivery, and postpartum as well as later, during perimenopause and menopause, hormones are underappreciated and can make ADHD feel like a rollercoaster.

According to Nadeau, female hormone changes and life transitional stages like puberty or pregnancy seem to exacerbate the symptoms of ADHD in women.

Internalizing difficult feelings and experiences—another trait of women with ADHD—causes anxiety and puts them at risk for self-harm and suicide. The founders of The Anxiety Sisters, an online community whose motto is "Don't go it alone," claim that it is typical to hear these admissions both online and in support groups.

Chapter 3

Strategies You Can Start With

There are numerous things a woman with ADHD may do to lessen the effects of her condition and have a more fulfilling life. Medication won't improve your life for you, but it can be helpful as you attempt to make changes. To begin creating a more ADHD-friendly existence, it may be good to engage with an ADHD specialist in solution-focused psychotherapy, but there are also many things you can do with friends, support networks, and more self-awareness.

Create or join a support group for women with ADHD.

The internal struggle is frequently the most difficult. Many women have been firmly entrenched with societal expectations. With others' help, breaking out of a mold of unrealistic expectations is simpler. Support groups for women with ADHD can be a great source of inspiration and empathy for women who are trying to lower their expectations for themselves and improve their coping mechanisms in the face of challenges.

Inform your loved ones about your ADHD and how it affects you.

An untidy home or disobedient kids may cause husbands to feel resentment and rage because they believe their wife "simply doesn't care." Her parents may react negatively, wondering why their daughter's home is messy and why she might require more emotional material, or financial support than their other children who do not have ADHD. Friends who do not have ADHD may mistakenly or purposely send negative messages. Work to inform all of your "significant others" about the effects of ADHD so they can support you and assist you in solving problems rather than criticizing and blaming you. Being a woman with ADHD is challenging enough without having to deal with supportive relatives and friends that hold you responsible for your problems.

Invite your partner to a local support group for adults with ADHD. Listening to other people with ADHD explain their struggles and marriages may often be eye-opening. When your husband hears other husbands discuss their marriages and the techniques they have discovered to live a calmer, better-managed life with their spouse, he may be more receptive to change.

Everybody's in the Family

Work to make your home an "ADHD-Friendly" space. If you have ADHD, there's a good chance that one or more of your kids also has. The frequency of emotional outbursts will reduce and you'll be able to save more energy for the positive aspects of life if you can accept your ADHD and that of other family members with good humor. Creating a home setting that is accommodating to ADD entails:

- Recognizing the sources of ongoing stress and making an effort to alleviate them, such as excessive commitment and persistent tardiness.

- Creating daily routines for your home will make going to sleep at night and waking up in the morning go more smoothly.

- For family members who are prone to emotional outbursts when under stress, provide "cool down places." Any area that is quiet, offers a comfortable spot to lie down, and has calm-down accessories like a soft music player, a cozy blanket, or possibly a stuffed animal for kids qualifies as a calm down zone.

- Be a family that solves problems rather than assigning blame.

- Learn to assign work based on preferences and strengths.

- Organize and declutter your space. Disorganization and clutter not only indicate stress, but also contribute to it.

If you need assistance creating an environment in your home that is conducive to ADHD, think about working with an ADHD coach or professional organizer.

Streamline your life.

Most women with ADHD have excessive schedules and commitments. Look for ways to lessen your own and your kids' responsibilities. Today's families are routinely overscheduled. Do not worry that by not attempting to keep up with the overschedulers next door, you are denying your child.

Get 30 minutes of aerobic activity each day.

Who has time for exercise? You may ask, but according to ADHD expert Dr. John Ratey, aerobic exercise is the single most crucial thing you can do to enhance brain function and lessen ADHD struggles. If you're unable to, you don't have to pay for expensive classes or join a gym. In fact, if you workout at home, it might be simpler to find a half-hour each day. Establish a routine. Studies have shown that exercise in the morning is more likely to be constant and that it is most likely to occur if it happens at a regular hour. The number of activities that can conflict with the time you set aside for exercise increases as the day progresses.

Try it for a week, doing it consistently every morning for 30 minutes. You'll notice that you are sleeping, concentrating, and feeling better.

Keep away from friends who are judgmental and don't comprehend your issues.

Find people who see the best in you and don't criticize you for your flaws. Finding this kind of companionship can start by signing up for a women's ADHD support group. The first time in their lives that they have been in a group of women who actually understand and accept their problems, according to many women with ADHD who participate in support groups. Try to stay away from ladies who will make you feel inadequate because of their exacting standards and unfavorable comparisons.

Include "time-outs" every day.

As stress relievers, time-outs are crucial. Married women with ADHD should request from their spouses that they assume full responsibility for the kids for a set period of time each weekend. Single mothers with ADHD should make every effort to schedule a dependable babysitter several times per week, and use these moments to relax. Make sure not to overbook yourself if you're a single lady with ADHD; schedule downtime.

Avoid becoming burned out.

One mother of two ADHD kids, who was excellent at raising her kids, was also able to admit her shortcomings. She made arrangements for a month-long summer sleepaway camp for each of her two difficult kids. She also planned quick trips to the grandparents, one at a time. As a result, she was able to spend time with each boy without worrying about his brother. Before you become exhausted, try to notice sensations of overload and look for methods to take a break. Mothers are not the only ones who experience burnout. If you have ADHD and are a single working woman, you may need to be careful to avoid working long hours without taking care of yourself. Many single career women with ADHD put a lot of effort into controlling their symptoms at work but utterly disregard their personal lives or an excessive focus on extracurricular activities. Single women must intentionally set aside time to unwind and recharge by "doing nothing."

Take away and assign.

In order to achieve better balance in their daily lives, women with ADHD must learn to minimize or delegate tasks. If you are a woman with ADHD, the organized chores of life are more difficult. One of the best investments you can make to create a lifestyle that is more stress-free and ADD-friendly is to spend more money on home help.

Parenting classes with a focus.

Parents of children with ADHD who are women with ADHD confront unique challenges and the difficulty increases if they are single parents. Children with ADHD are more difficult, require more guidance and assistance, and frequently have specialized educational and psychological requirements. It's critical to get support and education on how to work with and assist your child if he or she has ADHD. The "Parent to Parent" training groups offered by CHADD, a national organization that supports families affected by ADHD, are very affordable and can be very beneficial because they not only give you parenting tools but also the support and encouragement of other parents who truly understand the parenting challenges you face.

When a mother with ADHD misbehaves, it might be simple for other parents to condemn her from the outside looking in. However, as every parent of an ADHD child is aware, these children don't react the same way as typically developing children. You have a difficult job as a mother of a child with ADHD. Don't assign responsibility to yourself or let others criticize you. Instead, concentrate on receiving the guidance and assistance you require.

The significance of concentrating on what you love.

It is very simple to become so caught up in concentrating on the difficulties that come with having ADHD that you never allow yourself to concentrate on your skills, your attributes, and the things you enjoy. Your objective as a woman with ADHD should be to comprehend and embrace oneself. Try not to compare your achievements to those of others. Celebrate your ADHD's positive traits instead. The spontaneity, warmth, inventiveness, humor, sensitivity, and passion of so many women with ADHD are contagious. Work to create opportunities for being your best self as an ADHD woman, and seek out those who can see the best in you as well.

Be your cheerleader and give yourself a break.

Women who have ADHD are more likely to have despair, anxiety, and addictions as well as having more internalized symptoms. Think carefully about who you are and what you are worth. Even our classmates who are not adders make blunders. Be inquisitive, not enraged. To make your life more manageable, look for answers. Once you start being harsh on yourself, that might lead to even more guilt feelings. Strong negative reactions make it difficult to concentrate, act as self-fulfilling prophecies, and create a vicious cycle. Instead of dwelling on the past, practice mindfulness and accept each moment as it comes. If you find it difficult to confront your views on your own, think about cognitive behavioral therapy.

Chapter 4

Set Yourself Up For Success

Women with ADHD cover up their personality features by donning masks. Even when we're screaming within, we plaster on a grin and seem like everything is OK. Although hiding our genuine selves is difficult, we frequently believe that we have no other option.
Living honestly without covering up or making countless excuses is a process. Some people need counseling or the assistance of a life coach. Others find that simply accepting who they are, flaws and all, makes them feel more powerful. Whatever route you choose, keep in mind that you don't require "fixing." We're incredible, real women who are more than our transgressions or symptoms of ADHD. Trust the process, believe in

yourself, and have faith in your power because it has always been there.

Rekindle your aspirations. When you were a young girl, what did you want to become? How about when you were a young adult with ideals or a teenager? As we become older, we often lose sight of these dreams, but they are a part of who we are, and they can help women with ADHD become the best versions of themselves. Find some of your long-forgotten dreams then start making tiny progress toward realizing them. This does not imply that you should give up your job and pursue a career as a dancer! It can be anything as simple as borrowing a book from the library; perhaps you are still passionate about marine biology after all. It can entail joining a social sports team or organizing a trip to a fascinating new destination. Whatever you do, be sure it helps you reach your potential and provide a path to new chances.

Always remember you know what it is to persevere in difficult circumstances, you work twice as hard as everyone else simply to keep a sense of normalcy. A lot of individuals with ADHD don't give themselves enough credit for having this resilience, which is a major strength so always appreciate this beautiful part of you.

www.ingramcontent.com/pod-product-compliance
Lightning Source LLC
Chambersburg PA
CBHW060926130726
48001CB00006B/2432